Relevance: Black Men In Their Words About America

Dr. Angela Banner Joseph

illustrated by
Rituparna Chatterjee

Front Cover Layout: **Stanley Joseph Leslie**
Illustration: **Rituparna Chatterjee**

ISBN-13: 978-1943945023

ISBN-10: 1943945020

Library of Congress Control Number: 2016902664

Publisher: **Dr. Angela Marie Joseph**
New York City, NY

Copyright © 2017 by Dr. Angela Banner Joseph.
All rights reserved. No part of this book may be produced or utilized in any form or by any means- electronic or mechanical, digital, including photocopying, recording, or by any information storage or retrieval system, transmitted, or otherwise be copied for public or private use without written permission from the publisher. Inquiries should be addressed to Dr.AngelaJoseph@gmail.com

Printed in the United States of America

Also by Dr. Angela Banner Joseph

Two Nickels Holding Up a Dollar
I AM
Teaching Charlie the Value of a Dollar
YO SOY
Girls Breaking the Mold

Dedication

*This book is dedicated to my son
Stanley Joseph Leslie
and nephew Edwin L. Cancryn, Jr.*

Introduction

This book, *Relevance: Black Men in their Words About America*, is the story of the impact of living in a Black skin in American communities. The words of prominent men in America speak volumes about the experience of living and surviving as a Black male in America. This book is important for me to write because I am the parent of a man of color in America. I am conscious of his journey and his struggles as well as of the negative stereotypes he has experienced, from childhood through adulthood, while remaining active and whole. I am aware that his survival has not been easy, but he stands on the shoulders of great kings in the African Diaspora. Such men have shown society that he and others like him deserve respect.

What has happened to the Black man's voice in America? I am aware of what has happened, so I decided to take my love of quotations to weave a story using words of prominent Black men in America. Their voices examine how they have been treated and how they have felt to walk as a man of color on this planet. I have taken quotations from 12 people as threads in the story. The excerpts highlight many of the issues faced by Black boys and men in America: a breakdown of the family struggles with the educational system, elevated unemployment rates, drug abuse, crime and violence by and upon members of their race, and high incarceration rates.

Many Black youths have experienced the psychological, emotional, and spiritual consequences of low expectations, lack of self-confidence, and negative stereotypes about their behaviors. Too many have been labeled as criminals, seen as thugs, or perceived as dangerous. Others faced institutional racism such as housing discrimination, lack of recognition by educators and employers, the sting of invisibility and being ignored by service providers, and a variety of inequalities that have influenced relationships with their peers and families. Such disparities have led to significant peer pressure for young Black men to succeed without the active mentors who once strengthened the Black community.

How can the community change negative perceptions concerning young Black boys and men in America?

- What can we do to create positive change for people of color in all communities?
- What can we do to reduce crime and homicide against each other?
- What policies must we put in place to strengthen public confidence in men of color?
- How do we encourage young boys to choose higher education?
- What can we do to overcome the negative perceptions other ethnic groups feel when they see Black boys or men?

Next, what actions can Black men and boys take to improve their lives?

- How will you increase your confidence and self-esteem?
- How will you take ownership of your actions?
- How will you remove yourself from negative situations?
- How will you find the motivation to do your best?
- How will you set realistic financial goals for you and your family?
- How will you ask for help?

I close by saying that if no one has ever told you he or she believed in you, I am telling you I believe in your potential. You are brilliant, talented, thoughtful, and a genius. You are amazingly kind and caring, but most importantly, you are relevant. You have a voice in America, so let me hear you roar. Go for it! Accomplish your dreams and love yourself while doing so. Thank you for being your authentic self.

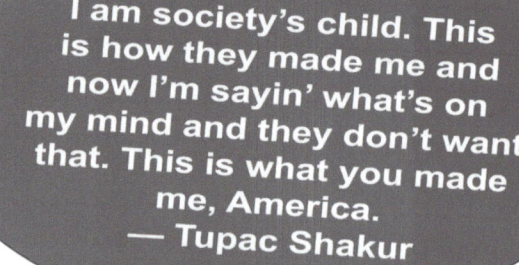

Black Men In Their Words About America

"I am society's child. This is how they made me and now I'm sayin' what's on my mind and they don't want that. This is what you made me, America. I am America. I am the part you won't recognize. But get used to me. Black, confident, cocky; my name, not yours; my goals, my own; get used to me. There's not an American in this country free until every one of us is free. I love America more than any other country in this world, and exactly for this reason, I insist on the right to criticize her perpetually. There's this big debate that goes on in America about what rights are: Civil rights, human rights, what they are? It's an artificial debate. Because everybody has rights. Everybody has rights-I don't care who you are, what you do, where you come from, how you were born, what your race or creed or color is. You have rights. Everybody's got rights. To be free…to walk the good American earth as equal citizens, to live without fear, to enjoy the fruits of our toll, to give children every opportunity in life—that dream which we have held so long in our hearts is today the destiny that we hold in our hands. Where justice is denied, where poverty is enforced, where ignorance prevails, and where any one class is made to feel that society is an organized conspiracy to oppress, rob and degrade them, neither persons nor property will be safe.

The United States has been called the melting pot of the world. But it seems to me that the colored man either missed getting into the pot or he got melted down. The common goal of 22 million Afro-Americans is respect as human beings, the God-given right to he a human being. Our common goal is to obtain the human rights that America has been denying us. We can never get civil rights in America until our human rights are first restored. We will never be recognized as citizens there until we are first recognized as humans. There is not a liberal America and a conservative America-there is the United States of America. There is not a Black America and a White America and Latino America and Asian America… there's the United States of America. I'm a black American, I am proud of my race. I am proud of who I am. I have a lot of pride and dignity. You are young, gifted, and Black. We must begin to tell our young, There's a world waiting for you, Yours is the quest that's just begun."

Quotes cited from *Tupac Shakur, Muhammad Ali, Jackie Robinson, James A. Baldwin, Julian Bond, Paul Robeson, Frederick Douglass, U.S. Supreme Court Justice Thurgood Marshall, Malcolm X, President of the United States, Barack Obama, Michael Jackson, and James Weldon Johnson.*

Further Reading

Tupac Shakur
http://www.biography.com/people/tupac-shakur-206528

Muhammad Ali
http://www.biography.com/people/muhammad-ali-9181165

Jackie Robinson
http://www.biography.com/people/jackie-robinson-9460813

James A. Baldwin
http://www.biography.com/people/james-baldwin-9196635

Julian Bond
http://www.biography.com/people/julian-bond-37971

Paul Robeson
http://www.biography.com/people/paul-robeson-9460451

Frederick Douglass
http://www.biography.com/people/frederick-douglass-9278324

U.S. Supreme Court Justice Thurgood Marshall
http://www.biography.com/people/thurgood-marshall-9400241

Malcolm X
http://www.biography.com/people/malcolm-x-9396195

President of the United States, Barack Obama
http://www.biography.com/people/barack-obama-12782369

Michael Jackson
http://www.biography.com/people/michael-jackson-38211

James Weldon Johnson
http://www.biography.com/people/james-weldon-johnson-9356013

Links retrieved from biography.com on January 24, 2017

Dr. Angela Banner Joseph was born in Belize, Central America and has been employed at the City University of New York School of Law since 1991 as Director of Financial Aid. She earned her doctorate from the School of Educational Leadership for Change at the Fielding Graduate University, Santa Barbara, California. Dr. Joseph received a Master of Arts degree in Urban Affairs from Queens College of the City University of New York and a Bachelor's Degree in Sociology from the State University of New York at Stony Brook. She lives in New York City.

ATTENTION: SCHOOLS AND BUSINESSES

Dr. Angela Joseph books are available at quantity discounts with bulk purchase for educational, business, or sales promotional use. For information, please email me at Dr.AngelaJoseph@gmail.com or visit Drangelabannerjoseph.com

www.ingramcontent.com/pod-product-compliance
Lightning Source LLC
Chambersburg PA
CBHW061402090426
42743CB00002B/112